**Written by Sandra Iversen**
**Illustrated by Pat Reynolds**

Jimmy can run
and Jimmy can jump
and Jimmy can play soccer.

He can read
and he can write
and he can paint.

Jimmy cannot hear Mom,
and Jimmy cannot hear Dad.

He looks at Dad's lips,
and he looks at Dad's hands.

Jimmy talks with his lips
and with his hands.
Jimmy likes to talk.

He cannot hear the cat
and the dog
and the car.

Jimmy hears with his eyes.
He looks at Mom's lips,
and he looks at Mom's hands.